SPAIN SINCE 1815

SPAIN SINCE 1815

BY HIS EXCELLENCY

MARQUÉS DE LEMA

ACADÉMICO DE LA HISTORIA
SPANISH MINISTER FOR FOREIGN AFFAIRS

A LECTURE DELIVERED AT THE LOCAL LECTURES SUMMER
MEETING, UNIVERSITY OF CAMBRIDGE, 1920

CAMBRIDGE
AT THE UNIVERSITY PRESS
1921

CAMBRIDGE UNIVERSITY PRESS
Cambridge, New York, Melbourne, Madrid, Cape Town,
Singapore, São Paulo, Delhi, Mexico City

Cambridge University Press
The Edinburgh Building, Cambridge CB2 8RU, UK

Published in the United States of America by Cambridge University Press, New York

www.cambridge.org
Information on this title: www.cambridge.org/9781107641181

First published 1921
Re-issued 2013

A catalogue record for this publication is available from the British Library

ISBN 978-1-107-64118-1 Paperback

SPAIN SINCE 1815

I

IT is difficult to include within the limits of a single lecture such an important period as that from 1815 down to the present day. Only a summary view of it can be offered by a lecturer who must naturally keep within certain bounds.

In the spring of 1814 King Ferdinand VII returned to Spain after his imprisonment at Valençay. During the period of the Peninsular War, called by Spaniards the War of Independence, extremely important events in the political history of the country had taken place. The Cortes, the Convocation of which Ferdinand VII himself while in Bayonne had ordered by a Decree of May 5th, 1808, at last assembled, although in a very different state from that which the monarch may have foreseen, for he doubtlessly believed it would retain its former legal form. Neither did the counsels of those prevail, who like the illustrious Jovellanos, because they thought it would be difficult for the Cortes to assemble according to the old Spanish usage, inclined to the constitution of two Chambers, having England's example before their mind's eye.

The Cortes which finally did assemble in Cadiz was an imitation of the French Constituent Assembly and those who were Deputies to it did not answer to the general political feeling of the nation but were under the influence of the Encyclopaedists of the eighteenth century and of the example of the French Revolution. This was the reason why in the middle of all their undeniable patriotism these Deputies proclaimed abstract principles and theories and wanted to put them into practice in spite of the country not being prepared for them and the fact that it was not the general will of the people that they should prevail. In this way when Ferdinand VII on his return, at the request of a great number of the ordinary Deputies to the Cortes of 1813, issued the Decree of May 4th, 1814, he undoubtedly gave satisfaction therewith to the majority of Spanish opinion. It was a grave error on his part that, not taking into account the patriotism of the men who had formed these Assemblies during his absence and looking only at their mistakes and at the attacks made on what he considered as his imprescriptible rights, he proceeded to imprison the most important Liberals of that period, and, not having obtained a sentence proportionate in his opinion to their delinquencies from the Tribunal set up to judge them, he punished them administratively by long terms of imprisonment or banishment.

On the other hand Ferdinand VII did not fulfil the promises made by him in the above-mentioned Decree, as he did not convoke the Cortes as he had offered to do according to the ancient public usage. It is thus that the period 1814–1820 has passed into history as an arbitrary period and one of obscurantism and bad Government, and not without reason. It is from this period that the widespread expression "Camarilla Governments" dates. It was in truth supposed that the King was ruled, not by the opinion of the Ministers who changed frequently but by that of a coterie which had its meetings in rooms not far from the Camara Regia, was composed of persons without responsibility, some of them being persons of lowly station, and succeeded anyway in intervening directly in the Government of the country.

The exact history of this period has not yet been really impartially and well investigated. It can, however, be affirmed that Ferdinand VII was not entirely controlled by his camarilla, but that this coterie often did succeed in interpreting the feelings and caprices of the monarch, and that he in his turn made use of the information obtained by means of this society for deciding the fate of his real Ministers.

It cannot be said either that the path taken by those who desired to overthrow the absolute Government of 1814–1820 was very much more reasonable or patriotic.

4

During the period of the French invasion the French armies had introduced some Masonic Lodges into Spain, which, although the invaders were expelled and those Spaniards who had joined the Napoleonic cause remained exiled, sprang up again under divers forms and with divers rites. The complete and without doubt curious influence exercised by the Masonic Societies on the happenings of that period still remains to be thoroughly studied, but it is evident that it penetrated into the rank and file of the Army and was an important factor in the political events of the time. For instance, as a result of the French invasion, Spanish power in America had considerably diminished and many of the kingdoms which formed that immense continent were in 1815 being undermined by ideas of risings and emancipation, if they were not in a state of complete rebellion. That is why it was necessary, after the return of Ferdinand VII, to think of the obligation to send help to the scanty armies which Spain had over there, awaiting the despatch of numerous forces to aid the Viceroys and "Captain generals" to overcome the insurrection. But if this idea was prevalent in Government spheres through the stern necessity which made itself felt, it was not thus in the Army, where there was a silent revolt concerning the crossing of the ocean and leaving the metropolis, fostered no doubt by the influence of some American personalities who desired to prevent troops being sent to America. Other influential elements in this action of the Masonic Lodges might have existed, but that these latter played an important part in the work of the demoralisation of the army, in order to prevent it being embarked for America, is a fact about which those who are thoroughly acquainted with this period entertain no doubts whatever. For example, when finally in 1819 it had become possible to get a sufficiently large army together from the towns of the present province of Cadiz, several conspiracies took place (in which some persons even took part of whose monarchical tendencies there had been no doubt), so that the de-

6

parture of the troops was delayed until at the beginning of 1820 the political movement openly broke out, which expressed the aspirations of the revolutionaries and which was aided by the resistance of the military elements against leaving the Peninsula. On the other hand, in what concerned the external affairs of Spain she did not see her just desires satisfied, as shewn in the meetings of the Vienna Congress, for Spain, after having been one of the most important bulwarks raised against the Napoleonic domination, did not obtain the consideration which certainly was due to her, either on account of the supineness of her representative at the Congress, or the want of real interest shewn by the Government of Ferdinand VII, or because of the unjustified forgetfulness of the Powers, some of which had bowed down before the Vienna Court, or perhaps on account of all these three reasons.

The ideas of the Holy Alliance must certainly have been agreeable to the Government circles, and with greater reason still to the King, who understood nothing of government except under the absolute forms which he considered as traditional, though they were without historical foundation.

Among the members of the "camarilla" there was a man of obscure origin who had found means of getting into the Russian Embassy. Ugarte (this being his name) succeeded in convincing the Court of the propriety of following the inspirations of the Muscovite Empire, and the Bailiff Tattischeff who represented that Court in Madrid became the most influential person as to external affairs with the Government of Ferdinand VII in the period from 1814 to 1820. One circumstance, however, contributed to diminish the prestige of the Russian Envoy and that was the acquisition of various ships, which were to aid the despatch of troops to America, from the Muscovite Government. These damaged frigates, the wood of which was rotten and which were of no service in the end, were remembered for many years to the discredit of the Bailiff and of the Government which

8

had let themselves be thus taken in and be induced to spend such large sums in spite of the pitiful state of the Spanish Treasury.

In January 1820 the first constitutional movement commenced which made the name of an obscure Major famous, called Rafael Riego. He was attached to the Asturias Regiment and had been one of those encamped near Cadiz in order to embark for America, but, undermined though the Army was, Riego together with other conspirators was not able to make more than a very small part of the Army join their cause, and it is certain that with another Government, a more energetic one and one more justified in public opinion, the movement would have proved an abortive one right from the commencement; but the want of serenity and energy in Ferdinand VII's Councils and the complicity of the Field-Marshal of Andalusia himself, the Irishman O'Donnell, the uncle of the still more famous General of the same name, placed the Government in a very difficult situation. But even then, if

9

the movements which took place in La Coruña in Aragon and later in Madrid had not sprung up, it is possible that the conspiracy might have been put down.

In view of these outbreaks Ferdinand VII on March 6th, 1820, agreed to convoke the Cortes in a form which would have to be prescribed later; but the following day, March 7th, precipitated thereto by the course of events and principally by the disagreement existing among those surrounding him, he promulgated a new Decree in which he accepted again the Constitution of 1812, which he had annulled on May 4th, 1814.

The second constitutional Government did not last more than three years in Spain and, to tell the truth, the errors committed were on a parallel with those of the absolute Government which had been replaced. The "clubs" and patriotic Societies stultified the efforts of these men who in good will had desired to give Spain an ordered Government and one which was sincerely constitutional. Soon after the establishment of the new system the greater part of the public opinion of the country trembled before the disorder to be seen in the policy and in the administration of the State. It is unnecessary to say that the monarch, even if he did give in to the demands of the new men whom he unwillingly called to form the State Government, at the bottom of his soul had no other feelings but that of anger and the desire to revenge the insults which he had received. We may say in passing that Ferdinand VII's character was the natural result of the alternate adulation and humiliation he had received. He had been brought up to a Court, in which, during the reign of Charles IV, that intimacy of relations which inspires naturalness had never existed between the King and Queen and the Infantes. Ferdinand, as Prince of Asturias, harboured a silent dislike of his mother, the Queen Maria Luisa, who on her side had not the proper love of a mother's heart for her first-born son. The future King of Spain had learnt the habit of dissimulation already in tender years.

Naturally clever, but poorly educated, since his boyhood he had reflected on the special position of Charles IV's Court in which the favouring of the Prince de la Paz profoundly wounded his feelings, for reasons which his apologists have never been able to analyse. Obliged to control these feelings which coincided with those nourished by the greater part of the Spanish people against the favourite, encouraged by the party which at the Court rallied to the side of the Prince, forced on many occasions anyway to bow down before the man whom he so strongly disliked, his character became so unequal and complex that even now it is difficult to differentiate the few good qualities possessed by Ferdinand from the grave defects which obscured his character.

Anyway, in the whole history of a country there has never been a monarch who enjoyed similar popularity. He was acclaimed by the nation at the time of his father's abdication with a jubilation which approximated to delirium. During the seven years of the War of Independence he became the

12

symbol of the national personality. Even after his imprudent conduct from 1814 to 1820, the errors committed by the Constitutional Governments again gave him back the halo, which he retained then to the time of his death, and which had not been missing during the first years of his reign.

The successive Ministries, one either more moderate or more exalted than the other, did not succeed in the period from 1820 to 1823 in putting a Constitutional Government into practice, under which the Royal prerogatives granted by the Constitution of 1812, which were so much reduced, were even respected. Ferdinand saw himself forced sometimes by the tumult raised by the partisans of one Minister at the doors, and even in the interior of his palace, to cancel Acts to which he had given his sanction on the advice of another Minister.

In the end the situation in Spain caused the attention of the European Powers to be called to it. Naples and Portugal had followed the example of the Spanish Revolutionaries, and though the movements in these

13

countries had been stopped long before by the efforts of the European nations the living example of Spain always remained, one which the Powers of the Holy Alliance could not recognise. For this reason the chief subject before the Congresses of Laibach and Verona was the situation in Spain and the necessity of overthrowing or of profoundly modifying her Government. Even England herself, which possessed constitutional institutions and which was obliged to oppose intervention in the internal affairs of Spain, was irritated thoroughly by the excesses committed by the dominating parties in Madrid and by the fight which it was necessary to promote in the north of Spain against the Monarchists who rose in arms to defend what they considered as being the vulnerated rights of the King. The French Government of Louis XVIII also put up a resistance against the impulses of the two European Empires and Prussia, which did not see any other remedy beyond the overthrowal of the Constitutional Government, though they did not wish to encounter the

14

opposition of England. When, however, at the end of 1822 the reports of the Representatives and French Agents brought the conviction to Louis XVIII and his Government that it was not possible for such a state of things to continue, the French monarch decided for intervention, and in his famous message to the Chambers of January 1st, 1823, he already demonstrated before his country what the motives were which induced him to defer to the request of the great European Powers.

In Madrid, in the middle of the political agitation, which, although fictitious in so far as the general opinion of the nation was represented, was serious enough to dominate the course of political events at that moment, the counsel of the moderate constitutionalists, which suggested the opportuneness of making certain reforms in the Constitution to pave the way for a *régime* acceptable to Europe, fell on deaf ears, and, among the inflammatory speeches made, the opinion of the most extreme party got the upper hand. When the French troops under

15

the Duke of Angoulême penetrated into Spain those patriotic spirits harboured the illusion that the country was bound to reply by driving them back in the same way as had been done years before at the time of the Napoleonic invasion, without taking into their calculations the fact that the institutions which existed in 1823 did not possess the same ardour as that of the high principles which had supported the throne of Ferdinand VII in the long and sanguinary fight against the powerful armies of the Empire. They succeeded, however, in carrying off the King by force to Seville, thus preventing the fall of Madrid coinciding with the overthrowing of the Constitutional Government, and when this refuge in the Andalusian city did not appear safe enough to them, and the King refused to go on to Cadiz, it was agreed at a meeting made famous by the pen of Alcalá Galiano, who played the principal part in the affair, to declare the King to be mad and to deprive him of his sovereignty, handing this over to a Regency.

It was only by this means that it was made possible to drag the monarch to Cadiz and to give him back the ghost of his authority as soon as he arrived inside the walls of that town. The sarcastic words of the King are still remembered which he spoke when a deputation of the Cortes communicated the re-establishment of his authority to him, confining himself to the ironical remark, "Therefore I am not mad now?"

The French armies did not lose much time in surrounding Cadiz, and the efforts of the scanty and badly organised troops which the Government desired to send against Louis XVIII's armies were completely unsuccessful in the other parts of Spain in view of the almost universal hostility of the country, the people of which received those whom they looked upon much as liberating forces with joy or at least with indifference.

On September 30th Cadiz being no longer able to withstand the siege, Ferdinand, already at liberty, went over to the French camp which had been set up at the

Puerto de Santa Maria. Unfortunately the rancorous feelings which had been smouldering for the last three years broke out into measures of severe and violent persecution, in spite of the prudent advice of the Duke of Angoulême himself, who, though desiring the re-establishment of the monarch's authority, was not a partisan of the excesses committed by an absolute and domineering Government.

The enthusiastic shouts with which the King was greeted on his return to Madrid, especially by the Monarchist volunteers, who differed in no way as far as their moral contexture was concerned from the National Militia of the previous period, confirmed him still more in the imprudent policy to which he committed himself at first. Not possessing a real army, fearful of reconstituting it and being aware of the ideas which predominated among the officers' corps of the army for the greater part and which had given rise to the events that we have just related, Ferdinand preferred the presence of the French Army for several years, during which time it was possible for him to organise new and loyal forces which would support his authority and retain his Crown for him. Thus the desire of the French Government of gradually diminishing the number of their troops in Spain, and the more intense wish of the other European Powers, especially England, to see this desire realised, were opposed by the will of the Spanish monarch, who was most anxious that the evacuation should be delayed as long as possible.

It would not be possible within the limits of one lecture to describe the various alternative occurrences of the second absolute period of Ferdinand's reign. It may be said that though the Government did not cease to be one without any parliamentary or popular intervention, when the first two or three years of the reaction had gone by, the events which took place, and in a certain measure also the greater enlightenment which had penetrated into the higher and governing classes, produced a relative moderation in the actions of the Government and

19

at the same time a certain tendency to improvement in the administration, which permitted this period to be called almost one of enlightened despotism. Another fact contributed to this, i.e. that the more extreme and irreconcilable part of the Royalist party, not content with the measures adopted against the Constitutionalists, whose chiefs had emigrated to other countries especially England or kept in the background or even accommodated themselves to the new state of things, considered that the King was badly advised in not following the inflexible line of conduct which they advised and attempted to group themselves round the Infante Don Carlos, whom, under the suggestion of a misunderstood religious spirit and in spite of his professed love for his brother, they set up as the head of a new party, known under the name of "Los Apostólicos."

A great number of the Royalist volunteers had continued to swell the ranks of the deteriorated Army with the approbation of the King, who thought to find in them the loyal forces which would support him. They, however, defended the intransigent policy of the Apostolic Party in such a way that at the end of 1827 they declared open rebellion in Catalonia, a rebellion which assumed such a terrifying character that for the first time Ferdinand was obliged to put himself at the head of his Army and loyal volunteers and to march to fight them on the same soil as where they had been raised.

But here more than ever it could be seen how, when out against both Liberal and "Apostólicos," the extraordinary popularity of the monarch's personality was retained, which, it may be said, was never lost at the bottom of the hearts of the Spanish people, in spite of his many errors and defects. His presence alone sufficed to dissipate the widespread and dangerous movement. During the journey, which lasted for about a year and which took the King through many of the Spanish provinces, it was made patent to the eyes of Europe, which looked on astonished how the "Beloved" ("Deseado") monarch retained that strange and powerful

21

influence, the want of which weighed down Spain during the horrors of the civil wars.

Ferdinand VII had been married thrice without any children to succeed him on the throne being born to him. When the death of the excellent Princess Maria Josefa Amelia of Saxony took place in 1829, he himself, sickly though not old, had to think about contracting another matrimonial union. He was moved thereto, not only by the natural desire of a man to possess direct descendants, but also by the expediency for the State that the Crown should not fall to the Infante Don Carlos, who was a good man but narrow-minded and of limited capacity. The latter thought himself invested with rights which nothing could violate in conformity with the laws then in force in the kingdom. It was any way certain that, in the Cortes of 1789 assembled to take the oath to the Prince of Asturias as heir to the throne, the Commoners asked the King, Charles IV, to annul the decision of the Supreme Court (Auto Acordado) of 1713 by which a monarch of

French origin, Philip V, had established the Salic Law in Spain, though in a somewhat attenuated form, which was in force in his own land. But this measure, which was so contrary to Spanish secular legislation, had not been invested with all the formalities which were necessary, as the vote of the Cortes had not been obtained. The Commoners of 1789 wished to return to the traditional system of the kingdom which gave to the females their never disputed right, and Charles IV consented, although for reasons which he considered weighty he retained the Decree dictated in agreement with the petition made by the Commoners without promulgating it. In consequence the only thing wanting in this Agreement which had been adopted by the monarch in the Cortes was its promulgation which could be carried out by himself or another monarch. And this is what Ferdinand VII did by means of the Pragmatic Sanction in April of 1830 in expectation of successors by his fourth wife, Maria Christina of Bourbon, daughter of the King of Naples.

His foresight was confirmed by events, for on September 30th of the same year Queen Christina gave birth to a Princess who would in time be the Queen Isabella II. But when she was sworn as heiress before the Cortes assembled in Madrid two years later, the King found himself up against the opposition of his brother the Infante Don Carlos, which was based on the conviction which he had of his own rights, aided by the influence of his wife, the Princess of Braganza, and of an undoubtedly powerful party.

Ferdinand saw himself forced in the last year of his life to send the Infante into exile, but did not succeed in making him abandon Portuguese territory. In this country the death of his royal brother came as a surprise to Don Carlos, for, although it had been expected, it was premature.

24

II

The situation of Spain at the death of
Ferdinand VII was critical in the last degree. So many ideas and passions in an
effervescent state, restrained only by the
strong personality of the late King, popular
with some though feared by others, could
not do otherwise than originate formidable
upheavals, in which the felicity and prosperity of the country were bound to suffer
grave harm. A youthful Queen, left a
widow with two little girls, and upholding,
perhaps without being fully aware of the
fact, the standard of the Liberals and Par-
liamentarians against the Absolutist *régime*
embodied in the Infante Don Carlos; a
powerful party attached to the cause of this
Prince and counting on 200,000 royalist
volunteers already under arms or prepared
to take them; a minority which was a minority, to be sure, but by no means an in-
significant one, by reason of the support it
derived from those who at that time were

25

called the Lights of the Century and who
were Constitutionalists, being Liberal and
Francophile *émigrés* who on Ferdinand's
death were envisaging the dawn of a new
day—the help of all these inevitably exerted
great influence over the Ministries of her
who had been proclaimed Queen-Regent;
yet another aggregation of eminent men
who, favouring an absolute though clement
monarchic system, were conscious of the
needs and changes of the time and from this
motive, as well as prompted by compas-
sionate feelings towards the fatherless and
otherwise unfortunate, likewise adhered to
the cause of Queen Christina and her small
daughters; and lastly as background to this
political and social *tableau*, masses of the
community who were equally as ready to
espouse with ardour the traditional *régime*
as to be won over by the flamboyant appeals
which were scattered broadcast by the revolutionary chiefs—these elements, fusing
together, constituted a whole that was
capable either of saving the country or of
plunging it into ruin, in proportion as it

was capable of being utilised, sanely directed, or controlled altogether.

The Queen-Regent possessed in her favour, notwithstanding the numerical inferiority of her partisans to those of the Pretender Don Carlos, and apart from the sentimental considerations to which I have referred, the advantage of having been *de facto* ruler during the last year of her royal husband's life, who after falling dangerously ill at La Granja in September of 1832, in the course of which illness he was now and then thought to be dead, had withdrawn from ruling and had entrusted the reins of government to his young consort. The latter, again, was regarded with sympathy and was supported morally, and afterwards even materially, by the two constitutional Monarchies of France and England respectively, whereas the Pretender received the support of the Central Powers, which support was less efficacious inasmuch as it proceeded from a remoter source.

The Will of Ferdinand VII had for its consequence the gathering round the throne of Isabella II of a number of important men, notwithstanding that many of these had hitherto and openly professed themselves Absolutists. And Christina had yet another advantage over her political rival the Infante Don Carlos, namely her beauty and graces of person, contrasting with the notorious deficiencies of the Pretender, such as his want of intelligence, his harshness of policy, and even of manners—deficiencies calculated to estrange from him and render of no account those elements, in themselves powerful, which had thrown in their lot with his fortunes. It was a matter of regret that the said influence and prestige of the Queen-Regent was lessened in the eyes of her subjects when these came to hear of her secret marriage, contracted a few months after the death of the King, to an officer of his bodyguard named Don Fernando Muñoz, who afterwards came to be known as the Duke of Riansares.

Though even prior to the death of Ferdinand the government had been entrusted to a man of moderate views within the

Absolutist party, namely to that prudent and diplomatic statesman Don Francisco Zea Bermudez, it was natural as well as unavoidable that upon the return to Spain of those noteworthy men who had created and cherished constitutionalism in the Cortes of Cadiz and in those held from 1820 to 1823, these same men should eventually come into power. Hence shortly afterwards, in 1834, a Government was formed on nakedly constitutional albeit moderate lines, whose president was the eminent statesman and man of letters, Don Francisco Martinez de la Rosa.

The same tendencies which had been outlined in men of the Liberal Party during the constitutional period of 1820 to 1823, manifested themselves in a bolder form while the new *régime* was maturing under conditions of liberty and without being subjected to interference by the Crown. Thus came into being the two classical parties of a Constitutional Monarchy, which then were called Moderates and Exalteds, this latter appellation being subsequently changed to

Progressives. Martinez de la Rosa, together with Isturiz, the Count of Toreno, and the Duke of Frias, projected a moderate constitutional system which should follow in the steps of the European movement in so far as the idiosyncratic conditions of the Spanish people would permit, and predisposed, in more ways than one, to innovations which gave offence to national sentiment. In particular their measures against the clergy and the religious establishments had alienated from the Spanish Liberals the support of many persons who otherwise would have found no difficulty in reconciling themselves to a moderate constitutional government.

The politicians aforesaid were perfectly alive to the fact that the Constitution of 1812, based upon the French Constitutions of the revolutionary period, even while it should respect religious unity, by impairing the Royal power in terms not ratified by later Spanish constitutions, could not operate without detriment to the Government itself and causing repulsion

30

among the inhabitants of the country at large.

For this reason Martinez de la Rosa set up a bi-cameral system by means of two bodies or assemblies, on which he bestowed the title of "estamentos," in order to give them a certain traditional appearance, at any rate in so far as their name was concerned. He caused to be voted and promulgated by these bodies a moderate constitution known as the "Estatuto." Nevertheless as he lacked sufficient power, because the outbreak of civil war had occasioned his government to be attacked in equal measure by the Carlists as by the Exalteds and Revolutionaries who detested the mildness of his conduct, he was unable to avoid such disgraceful episodes as that which was known as "The Massacre of the Friars," when drunken crowds committed all manner of horrors against defenceless clerics. After this the Government was unable to turn back in the direction of elements whose doctrines seemed to be those of sympathy with the partisans of the Pretender; consequently

the power could not do otherwise than pass
into the hands of the Extremists. Among
these a man was prominent who has left his
mark on Spanish politics, namely the famous
Mendizábal, Jewish by birth, financier and
financial agent of foreign banking houses,
and who now stood out among the advanced
politicians. Mendizábal projected and in
great part realised the plan summed up by
the laws of civil and ecclesiastic amortization. By these laws he was unquestionably
able to procure for the moment funds wherewith to carry on the war against the Carlist
forces and by means of a system of land
tenure he was able to create a number of
partisans deeply interested in conserving the
new political institutions. But at the same
time he misapplied funds which, had he
dispensed them slowly and methodically,
would have enabled him to avoid injury
to the susceptibilities of many classes of
the community, together with a rupture
lasting for many years with the Papacy.
By his acts he supplied moral weapons to
those persons who were antagonistic to the
32

Government of Queen Isabella and her mother, and in addition to all this he deprived the country of an enormously valuable source of revenue, whereupon the public estate might have been erected in a solid and satisfactory manner.

As soon as Mendizábal had begun this work, the uproar which rose against him, and the continued disturbances and risings in the Provinces, compelled the Queen-Regent to summon once more to power the moderate elements in the person of that eminent statesman who afterwards for long represented Spain at the English Court, namely Don Francisco Javier Isturiz. But three months later, when the Queen and her daughters were at the country palace of La Granja, a disgraceful conspiracy carried out by some soldiers and led by the notorious Sergeant Garcia, broke into the Royal apartments and compelled the Queen-Regent, on peril of her life, to dismiss the constitutional government and to proclaim under her signature the Constitution of 1812. These happenings, which were witnessed by the

English Minister, George Villiers, later on better known as the Earl of Clarendon, and who has given us an interesting description of them in his letters and memoirs recently published, cast upon Spanish politics a stain which could only be removed with difficulty.

The Queen and her daughters were compelled to return to Madrid surrounded by the same mutinous soldiery, and to raise to power persons who either supported and directed the revolutionary elements, or else were drawn away by these; but neither the Calatrava Ministry which was then formed, nor those cabinets which succeeded it, considered it possible to govern with the Constitution of 1812, and therefore in 1837 they voted a new political Code. While these events were happening at the Court, the forces of the Pretender advanced through divers provinces of Spain and at the close of 1836 they reached the very gates of Madrid. The exigent demands put forward by the revolutionary element deprived the Queen's forces of a leadership as competent as was

34

that which proved to be, little more than a year subsequently to his entering thereupon, the commandership of Don Luis de Cordova, the ablest military leader of all whom the Constitutional system produced. At the moment in question, however, everything was confusion and disorder, together with a depleted treasury.

At the beginning of 1837 Christina's position seemed to be well nigh desperate. Fortunately, however, by calling to the Councils of the Crown men of less extreme views, and by utilising the services as diplomats of other men such as the Marquis of Miraflores, who had played so important a part in the treaty of the Quadruple Alliance, signed in London in 1834, and assisted by the good fortune which accompanied the military operations carried out by Don Baldomero Espartero, who was the General newly placed in command of the Army, she succeeded little by little in improving the situation of the Constitutional Monarchy. Another source of assistance was the disorder and discord which broke out in the camp of

35

Don Carlos himself. Moreover, the nation was wearying of the destruction involved by so lengthy a war and by so many revolutions, which, in addition to the enormous damage they inflicted on the country, kept up an agitation and effervescence which were wholly incompatible with all progress.

Even greater were the effects caused by this state of things in the Pretender's camp and in those provinces in the north where the military operations for the most part took place. The quarrels between the Pretender's Generals, whereof the Liberal leader took advantage, and the work cleverly carried out in Paris by the Marquis of Miraflores, had for their result that in 1839 a great part of the Carlist Army, led by General Maroto, accepted the Agreement concluded at Vergara. The Carlist General and General Espartero embraced at the head of their forces. This Agreement practically put an end to the Carlist insurrection, although during the remainder of that year and throughout 1840 a good deal of military effort was needed to get the insurrection completely under, especially in Aragon and Catalonia, in which provinces the celebrated Cabrera continued to maintain a remarkably obstinate and vigorous resistance.

Espartero, having thus proved victorious, naturally constituted himself the arbiter of Spanish politics. A man of mediocre talents as a politician, and under the influence of those around him, he failed to realise that which would have conferred upon his name an imperishable renown, namely, the fact that he had maintained himself superior to party influence and had thus served as a bond of union between them all, while faithfully remaining beside the throne of Isabella II and her royal mother. Instead of envisaging this fact, he preferred to place himself at the head of one of these parties, namely the Progressive, and formed ambitious plans whose consequence was that in September of 1840 Queen Christina quitted Spain and a regency was set up by himself, now known by the title of Duke of La Victoria. It is true that a contributory cause was the loss of prestige

37

which the Queen-Regent had suffered by
reason of a marriage, which was secret and
yet known or suspected by all, and which
effectively deprived her of the necessary
legal conditions for discharging her exalted
trust.

Melancholy indeed was that stage of
Spain's history wherein the ambitious de-
signs of military men, supported by con-
tinuous *pronunciamientos*, rendered it impossible to make a worthy use of the triumph
which had been secured over the Absolutist
cause of Don Carlos!

No sooner had General Espartero taken
upon himself the regency than a powerful
movement was set on foot against him by
many elements which had remained loyal to
the deposed Queen-Regent, and particularly
by certain Generals among the most distinguished who had taken part in the Civil
War. Prominent among these were Don
Leopoldo O'Donnell, then Count of Lucena,
who had shone during the campaigns carried
out in the east of Spain and in Aragon and
Catalonia, and also Don Ramon Narvaez,

the pacifier of La Mancha and Andalusia, who moreover was gifted with great energy and conspicuous political talent.

The Regent succeeded in quelling the first movement of this upheaval and caused to be shot certain distinguished Generals, including one or two whose achievements in war had made them almost legendary. Of such was Don Diego de Leon. Nevertheless, it may truthfully be said that conspiracies did not cease during the three years of the regency of the Duke of La Victoria, until finally they threw him from power in 1843. He was obliged to take ship for England, where as an *émigré* he replaced many members of the Moderate party who had been forced to leave Spain when Espartero himself had been raised to the pinnacle of power.

From 1843 to 1854 there predominated, among various other forms of government, the Moderate party, whose leader-in-chief was the aforesaid General Narvaez. This period is a bright one in the annals of Spanish politics of the 19th century, because, after the Crown Councils had been augmented by men of considerable knowledge and exceptional talent, such as Pidal, Pacheco, Mon, Pastor Diaz, and others, there dated hencefrom those forms of civil and administrative organisation, which with minor alterations continued to dominate the remainder of the century.

A matter of a domestic character, but yet which provoked a great stir in other countries, was the marriage of Queen Isabella, whose majority had already been recognised although her age was only fourteen, and the marriage of her sister the Infanta Doña Luisa Fernanda.

When we glance into the past and call to mind how chancelleries worried and toiled over the matter in question and the suspicions that were aroused in connection therewith, we find it difficult to understand so mighty a to-do in connection with an affair which realities rendered of no importance whatever in European history. The vanity and perishableness of all human enterprises are surely well illustrated by the fear at that time experienced by the Powers, and particularly by Great Britain, lest France should acquire too great an influence by the marriage of the Queen of Spain to a member of the family of Louis Philippe; for within two years after that marriage had been celebrated Louis Philippe lost his throne as well as this matter of state its main point of interest. After the King of France had declared his resolve to withdraw his sons' names as candidates for the union aforesaid, various other candidates came forward, including a son of Count Trapani, a German prince, and several Infantes of Spain, inasmuch as rivalries existed over this matter even within the family of Don Francisco de Paula, younger brother of Ferdinand VII. Finally, in October of 1846, Queen Isabella married her cousin the Infante Don Francisco de Asis, while her sister, the Infanta Doña Luisa Fernanda, became the wife of the Duke of Montpensier, younger son of King Louis Philippe.

Rivalries and jealousies thus overswept Europe. But that which all nations forgot was to take thought for the happiness of the youthful Queen and for the welfare of the Spanish Nation. It is beyond doubt that this forgetfulness was succeeded, during the reign of Isabella II, by appreciable consequences of a political nature giving rise to happenings substantially harmful to the peace and well-being of Spain herself.

The energetic policy of the Moderate Government at the head of Spanish affairs in 1847, and especially that which was shown by its President, General Narvaez, warded off from Spain the misfortunes brought upon other European countries by the Revolution of 1848. In this context it is worth while to recall the particular position of those two nations with which Spain has ever maintained the closest relations with regard to her own domestic affairs. Speaking on general lines it may be stated that the representatives of Great Britain, guided by the policy which Lord Palmerston had initiated and by the greater ease wherewith they found themselves able to treat with the Progressives, preferred to seek within this party their support for the policy exercised by Great Britain at that time.

As long as the British Legation was entrusted to the Lord Clarendon that was to be, this gentleman, notwithstanding that his sympathies leaned towards the policy we have mentioned, maintained a friendly bearing towards all of our parties alike. But others of Great Britain's Representatives, notably Mr Bulwer, carried to an extreme pitch their interference in our domestic affairs, and always on the side of the Progressive party. This led to an incident which caused a great stir at the time, for General Narvaez, being convinced that Mr Bulwer had been playing the intermeddler in Spanish politics and had been helping those whom the General adjudged to be pro-revolutionary, handed him his passports and asked him to leave the kingdom. However, so cogent were the reasons which backed up the Head of the Spanish Government, that after the necessary explanation had been tendered, the incident provoked no disturbance of the friendly relations existing between Spain and

Great Britain, united to which was the intervention in Portuguese affairs with the object of upholding the rights of Doña Maria de la Gloria.

As a reaction from this policy exerted by the Representatives of Great Britain in favour of the Progressive party, the Spanish Moderates courted the intelligence and encouragement of the French Government, and this improper intervention of one and the other foreign power necessarily gave rise to many incidents in the politics of Spain, always in greater or less degree disturbed by the various influences at work round the young Queen. Yet all this notwithstanding, the Moderates succeeded, as we have stated, in governing for a long period on lines that were obviously beneficial to the quiet and prosperity of Spain.

Apart from legislative improvements, those of an administrative character, and those relating to finance, this period was marked by the inauguration of enterprises that were indispensable to the development of production and the national wealth.

44

Unfortunately there existed among the Moderate Party certain rivalries, as shown in the case of the Government formed by Señor Bravo Murillo in 1850 to 1852. It is true that this statesman, whose gifts were in many ways remarkable, took up an idea which at that time was hovering about the Court, and which was promoted into hard fact by the triumph in France of the *coup d'état* of December 2nd, 1851, which had for its virtual effect the removal of constitutional and parliamentary representation by introducing into the Constitution of 1845 reforms of such a character that, had they taken root, would almost have rendered it null and void.

The same Government was prompted by tendencies of a well-meaning nature but devoid of practicality in the circumstances then obtaining. For example, it sought to lessen military influence in the national administration. But that which is inefficacious by its own character invariably leads to results very different from what its authors had intended. Thus it happened that the most

45

prominent army-generals, on perceiving the plans to remove them from political life, united with one or another of various parties, and especially with the Moderates, in order to overthrow a Government which to some extent seemed to be repeating the French *coup d'état*.

On the fall of Bravo Murillo's Ministry, this was succeeded by several Governments which had only a short life, but the same tendencies persisting on the part of the same politicians who had formed part of the said Bravo Murillo Ministry plunged the country into a lamentable state of affairs, insomuch that, in 1854, directed by the eminent General Don Leopoldo O'Donnell, and with the good will, or even the active assistance, of others, including General Narvaez himself (notwithstanding that he personally kept aloof from the movement), there came about one of the most momentous and far-reaching *pronunciamientos* of the reign of Isabella the Second. After O'Donnell had been overthrown at Vicálvaro by the Government troops, the consequences became even worse, because the authors of the *pronunciamiento*, seeing the failure thereof, considered it necessary to solicit the help of the old Progressive party and of their leader General Espartero, who, since returning from England a few years previously, had lived in seclusion in La Rioja. Now was witnessed the spectacle of a Court which, notwithstanding that its government had mastered the revolutionary outbreak, yet found itself obliged to temporise with those factionists who had converted Madrid and other parts of Spain into a stage for events which already seemed to have been forgotten, and this with the concomitant circumstances, equally strange, that those elements, reputedly moderate, which had started this revolution, united with the Progressives under the presidency of the Duke of La Victoria and began from the very first moment to undermine the same situation which they themselves had helped to create.

The successful revolution of 1854 presented the novelty in Spanish history of the last century that it brought to light certain new elements, which taking the name of democrat began to exercise influence in politics; and these elements it was which years later played the leading part in the revolution of 1868 which overthrew the throne of Queen Isabella. Those who formed these elements consisted for the most part of young men of great enthusiasm and possessing greater talent than the already outworn Progressive Party, and they were animated by the tendencies which had been developed in Europe by the Revolution of 1848. Consequently they ambitioned a wider horizon than was offered to their view by the group led by the Duke of La Victoria, which group merely aimed at being in power, while clinging obstinately to administrative theories which nearly broke down in actual practice.

In this strange amalgamation the Progressives and Moderates of the old school, who made up between them the Government known in Spain as the Biennial Progressive of 1854 to 1856, were overthrown in the latter year by the counter-revolution

48

which the moderate elements both inside and outside of the Government and also a great part of the Army had been preparing under the direction of the originator of the Revolution of two years previous, namely General O'Donnell, at that time Minister for War. The success O'Donnell met with at this second working of his political combination, led to the formation of a party which, containing at the same time Moderate and Progressive elements, governed Spain for quite a long period and was called the Liberal Union. Its leader, O'Donnell, achieved that which appeared impossible in those days of short-lived and even ephemeral ministries, inasmuch as he framed a policy which governed the country for five years, a brilliant and successful proceeding, but which was unable to provide a solid gubernatorial system, to a great extent because his party rested on a purely personal basis. However, for a number of years, O'Donnell was well supported among the Army, while the Spanish people, trusting in his prestige, regarded his government as a guarantee

M. DE L.

of an ordered and prosperous state of affairs.

O'Donnell cemented cordial relations with the Papacy, which relations, after having been renewed by the Concord of 1851, had been again broken off during the term when the Progressives were in power. By this means he succeeded in settling once and for all that grave question touching the rights of conscience which represented in the eyes of many Spaniards the amortization of church property, and he secured to owners of national property the possession of what they had acquired in return for compensations respecting the maintenance of religion and the clergy, which said compensations had been offered to the Holy See. Another remarkable circumstance concerning this period was also the fact that by making use of the best administered portion of the civil and clerical disamortization, which had the effect for the time being of making the public treasury appear to flourish, large sums could be expended for military purposes, both in reorganising the Army and in fortifying towns and coasts, as well as in building warships; indeed, the "Numancia" was the first protected frigate to sail right round the world.

The so-called African War, although its results eventually proved to have been of trifling importance, contributed in a great measure to enhance the brilliancy of that period in our political life, and afforded a truce, so to speak, during which our political passions quieted down and the patriotism of our nation was reawakened. With an army relatively small in number and notwithstanding that the expedition was not regarded favourably by Great Britain (which, unlike the Imperial Government of France, impeded the action of our Government by all manner of obstacles) we were able, nevertheless, by means of our troops, who otherwise would have entered Tangier by land, to overcome the Moorish Army led by Muley-el-Abbas, brother of the Sultan, and to conquer Tetuan and dominate the part of these territories, which is now a Spanish Protectorate. We were also able to overcome a quasi-Carlist conspiracy which the sons of the Pretender Don Carlos sought to turn to their own advantage. With apparent success, too, the Spanish Government effected the ill-advised annexation of Santo Domingo and the expeditions to Mexico and Cochin-China side by side with France and England. Nevertheless, in the Mexican expedition Spain and Great Britain worked together in perfect accord and by this means were able to steer clear of those formidable rocks on which the French Empire was shattered to pieces.

With respect to the Spanish political situation of those days, there was taking place something which, at a longer interval and on a far greater scale, characterised the second Napoleonic Empire. Everything appeared to be more brilliant than it really was. Solidity and finality were lacking, in such wise that when the warmth of political passions and party intrigues occasioned the temporary fall of O'Donnell, and certain events in our politics, such as the annexation of Santo

Domingo, turned out in the long run to have been serious failures, O'Donnell's prestige, as well as that of the important party whose leader he was, suffered considerably. Yet even then popular trust was reposed in the influence, believed to be impregnable, exerted in Army circles by the first Duke of Tetuan (O'Donnell having been honoured by this title after the African campaign), and it was thought that the unfortunate period of *pronunciamientos* had been brought to a close. Nevertheless, when the Duke, from 1865 to 1866, formed his last Ministry including several of Spain's most eminent politicians, such as Zabala, Bermudez de Castro, Calderon Collantes, Alonso Martinez, and Canovas del Castillo, there took place the sanguinary occurrences of June 22, 1866, constituting the most formidable revolution which had afflicted us in the course of many years. At the head of it was General Prim, and, although it was completely overcome by the Government, the days of the Liberal Union were already numbered. By a policy of repression

53

the Crown and part of the country understood that the remains of the old Moderate Party were best suited to stand at the head of affairs. Hence, in July of 1866, and also for the last time there came into power General Narvaez, Duke of Valencia. Nevertheless this view, although it seemed to be logical, brought disaster upon the throne of Isabella II, because most of the members of the Liberal Union, considering that they had been very ungratefully treated by the Queen, at the same time that their favour was solicited by the Progressives and Democrats, only resisted the appeal then made to them as long as General O'Donnell was alive; for he never forgot for one moment his loyal obligations towards the Throne. But at his death on November 5th, 1867, the Moderate Government carried its repressive measures to the last extremity, whereupon all parties united against the one in power, in such manner that after Narvaez had also died in March of 1868, the Revolution now feeling its strength, and furthermore being but feebly withstood, was

54

able in September of that year to overthrow the Throne of Queen Isabella and to open a new period in Spain's political history.

If we consider these important political events in the light of the results accruing therefrom, we may truthfully say that whatever may have been the deficiency of the *régime* which was in force throughout the reign of Isabella II, and whatever the personal defects of the Sovereign, her dethronement assuredly was not beneficial to the country. At the moment when the revolution of 1868 broke out, Spain was still a nation which counted for something in the Councils of Europe. As a naval power her position was fourth on the list. During the previous twenty-five years of Isabella's reign, the country had benefited substantially in the material sense, since harbours had been constructed, railroads laid, and means of communication generally had been greatly improved. The public debt, notwithstanding our civil commotions, had been lessened, so that in regard to national finance our position was relatively normal.

The six years which intervened between the fall of Queen Isabella and the restoration of the dynasty in the person of her son, were, on the other hand, marked by events which damaged Spain's national life and her credit. It is open to discussion whether the development, which according to some persons took place in our social and political ideas, constituted a real forward step or not. Certain it is that, in so far as this development was lawful and desirable, these benefits would have been obtained without the throes of that period of revolution, in the course of which Spain witnessed the Regency of General Serrano, Duke of La Torre, the short-lived monarchy of Don Amadeo of Savoy, and a calamitous interval of republican government, whose existence scarcely lasted a year. Then came the moderate Government of 1874, which served as an anticipation of and a preparation for the monarchical restoration desired by the majority of the country.

During these six years there raged a new and terrible civil war, because the Carlists, who, if the Bourbon dynasty had not been interrupted in their occupation of the Throne, would certainly not have lifted up their heads once more, and if the delicate religious problem had not again come into being, took up arms on seeing an attack directed against those principles which they held to be essential and salutary. This civil war did not spread all over Spain as the first one had done, but, although it was limited to the Northern Provinces and Catalonia, it cost the country thousands of lives and the loss of enormous wealth. At the same time too there broke out Federalist and even Anarchist risings in the south and east, together with the first Cuban War, which also occasioned immense loss of life and wealth and was the forerunner of the second Cuban War which ended in the severance of Spain from her rich overseas provinces, the last remains of the great colonial Spanish Empire. Consequently there is no need to dwell upon the condition in which our country found herself at the time when, by an almost unanimous act proceeding from the Army, and which did no more than anticipate, perhaps needlessly, a measure which the Spanish Cortes would themselves have adopted, the Prince of Asturias, son of Queen Isabella, was proclaimed King of Spain under the title of Alfonso XII.

III.

The Restoration of the Monarchy at the close of the year 1874, as well as the subsequent march of Spanish politics, belong to a period well known among its contemporaries, and even better known among the distinguished audience to which this address is delivered. The said Restoration of our Monarchy connotes in the minds of Spaniards an epoch of pacification, inasmuch as within one year after it had taken place the Civil War was definitely brought to a close by the overthrow of the Carlist forces, and within two years the Cuban Insurrection was likewise suppressed.

The political *régime* set up by the new Constitution promulgated in 1876, having for its object the embodiment of everything contained in the preceding codes that was serviceable from the national standpoint, continues in force at this present day. Furthermore, it may also be said to be respected without discussion, a marvel that had never been witnessed in the whole course of last century. National administration was set in order, while by regularising our finances and developing the productivity of the country we were enabled to promote by degrees an economic condition of relative prosperity. Even if certain vicissitudes befell, such as are inherent in all human affairs, not one of them, excepting those which were beyond the scope of mortal provision and care, such as the untimely death of Don Alfonso XII, diverted from their calm and natural flow institutions which the nation had come to regard as essentially its own. Even the melancholy circumstances under which the deceased monarch was succeeded by his as yet unborn son, in the days of the Regency ably exercised by Queen Maria Christina, followed their course without public order being in the smallest degree disturbed, far differently than would have been the case in other times and other countries; and this fact notwithstanding that minorities have never been unattended by danger.

The closing years of last century were marked by only one happening of major importance. I refer to the loss of the last remains of our Colonial Empire, the final and by no means the least mournful episode of our tragic history. Nevertheless the nation bore up against this blow without its domestic affairs being in any way troubled and without any diminution of its growing prosperity. In fact the shock of this tragic event was presently succeeded by pious oblivion, and, later on, even by feelings of cordial friendship towards the very same newborn Republic which had followed the same path of emancipation which aforetime had been trod by vast regions that once were a flower in Spain's coronal. And even our justifiable feelings of resentment towards that mighty Power, situated in America, without whose assistance it is possible that Spain might not have been definitely severed from the last remaining of her colonies, have grown milder in face of the conviction on our part that the fatal and inevitable hand of destiny would in any event have consummated the material severance of Spain from the boundless American Continent; but which, notwithstanding such severance, will always be linked to the old Mother Country by bonds of a spiritual kind.

Renewing the course of history, interrupted for four centuries, a law of nature has extended the action of Spain to the continent of Africa, and although the portion thereof allotted to Spain is of relatively tiny dimensions, it is our hope and belief that the modesty of our ambitions and the always cordial relations we have maintained with the British Government, whose collaboration Spain was at no time willing to forgo, even at moments when she could have done better for herself by concluding agreements elsewhere, portend a happy and speedy consummation of the negotiations now proceeding for the definite settlement of the problem of Morocco.

The course of Spanish politics subsequent to the felicitous Restoration of the Monarchy under Alfonso XII, during the Regency of Queen Maria Christina, and the reign of her August Son Don Alfonso XIII, has been influenced by many men of mark, whose names are so familiar that there is no need to bring them to mind. In one case, however, I feel it incumbent upon me to make an exception by referring to the most illustrious of all Spanish statesmen of the constitutional era, namely Don Antonio Canovas del Castillo. To him were due the credit for the work of preparation, as well as for the successful direction thereof, which preceded the Restoration of the Monarchy; and also for the broad and generous-minded Constitution which still obtains in our midst. To him, once more, Spain owes the tolerant yet withal practical present *régime*. He, too, was the first to realise the grave economic problem involved in the due safe-
62

guarding of our national interests conjoined to our rivalry with other countries. He, it was yet again, who grasped the importance of our social problems and embarked upon a course of reform which at first the predominant individualism sought to withstand; and he who successfully invoked the co-operation of politicians of all shades, even those who derived from the revolutionary ranks or monarchists of the Extreme Right. He, once again, maintained the defences and resistance of Spain face to face with the Cuban Insurrection, while at the same time bestowing upon that island reformative measures which conceivably might have satisfied the aspirations of the Cubans and thus have averted the severance of the bonds which united them to the Mother Country, had not the operation of those reforms been intercepted by the intervention of the United States. It is also beyond question that, had he not met his death at the assassin's hand, he would have discovered a suitable solution of the grave international conflict which hung over Spain, and whose ultimate phase

63

was the Spanish American War. In establishing two great political parties, the Conservative and the Liberal, Canovas was supported by another statesman of eminence, namely Señor Sagasta, the Liberal leader, the union of which parties has permitted, during a period of thirty years, the tranquil and ordered play of our political institutions, in such manner that, notwithstanding inherent deficiencies and errors which are easy of comprehension, the country was governed with a sureness and firmness hitherto completely unknown.

Within the necessarily restricted limits of an isolated address, it is hardly possible to consider Spanish history from 1815 onwards otherwise than from the standpoint of general politics, inasmuch as any examination of our national development under other headings would have entailed fatiguing an audience by its very length. Consequently I am debarred from even so much as tracing the important literary and scientific movement which proceeded during the

19th century, and even in greater degree our industrial and commercial development. That which cannot be undertaken properly had better not be attempted. Nevertheless, permit me to add, by way of conclusion, a few brief remarks concerning Spain's social and political development.

Whosoever observes the political changes which Spain has undergone in our own time will assuredly have noted one fact that surprised him. The changes in question were not the outcome of a lengthy elaborative process such as that of the English Constitutional system, nor were they brought about sharply and spasmodically, imposing themselves from the very first and consolidating themselves with firmness, as in the case of the *régime* set up in France by the Revolution of 1789. In Spain there were no reasons why a revolution on an important scale should triumph swiftly and definitely. That which began in the first years of the 19th century was an imitation of what had taken place in France; but its antecedents were not of the same character. Even in times of the Absolute Monarchy the predominant characteristic of Spain's social and political life was a real and widespread democracy. The conviction that their kings had been the staunchest defenders of the people against the nobility and the foreigner was always present in the minds of the Spaniards, and notwithstanding that since the reign of Charles V the power of the Cortes was reduced by the withdrawal therefrom of the nobility and clergy from the year 1537, these Cortes were convoked during the 16th and 17th centuries, there being present the Procurators of Cities who succeeded at times in restraining and even in frequently obstructing the political acts of the Sovereign, by reason of their opposition to granting supplies.

It was not until the 18th century that the Cortes ceased wholly to meet, except when monarchs and their heirs were proclaimed or took the oath; but at all times and both under the Austrian and Bourbon dynasties, the Spanish people always considered themselves at liberty to address complaints to their Sovereigns, whenever they considered that the ministers of these were guilty of measures they deemed harmful to the public weal.

Again, when the Spanish nobles had been stripped of their old-time power and derived their only lustre from their nearness to the Throne, there remained between them and the people none of that hostility which is a characteristic of other countries.

Once more, the Spanish Court was never the scene of open dissipation of a kind such as to stir the repulsion of the people and provoke their protest. The greatest libertine among Spain's kings, namely Philip IV, never flaunted his failings before the multitude, and the straitlaced usages and etiquette of the Court consequently suffered no harm thereby.

The Bourbon Kings, again, were good-living men, especially Charles III, whose simplicity and excellent morals caused him to be looked upon as one of the most venerated sovereigns in Spanish history. This explains why, when during the reign of his son, Charles IV, the people noticed a falling off in the standard of Court life, although not in the monarch himself, they directed their irritation against the person they considered to blame, and particularly against the Favourite, whom not without reason they considered to be under the sway of vices unknown in the history of the Spanish Monarchy.

The French invasion of 1808 occasioned days of heroism and glory for the Spanish people, who in alliance with England succeeded in driving out the usurper after seven years of sanguinary struggle, but this struggle had grave consequences in that it precipitated the separation of Spain from her American provinces, and also in Spain's internal affairs because certain well-intentioned people who had become obsessed by French teaching, but who were unable to understand the real state of affairs, availed themselves of the crisis when Spain was struggling for her life against Napoleon and established amidst artificial surroundings a *régime* and a constitution which was no more than an

68

imitation of the French Constituent Assembly. On effecting this, the persons aforesaid wounded feelings that were deeply implanted in Spanish bosoms and roused to wrath the captive King, who, without deserving it, was regarded by the nation as their idol, and who, in their eyes, stood both for the cause of their independence against the foreign invader and against the intriguing of court favourites such as were ever abominated by the Spanish people. Thus was presented the curious spectacle that in the ordinary Cortes of 1813, resulting from the Constitution of the preceding year, a large number of deputies solicited from the King on returning from his captivity the abolition of the very Constitution whereby had been elected the very Assembly to which they themselves belonged.

Ferdinand VII lacked the serenity and elevation of view which were so essential in those days, and the example of prudence and judgment set him by his kinsman, King Louis XVIII of France, was lost upon him. The Spanish Constitution, under the influence of this time, could not do otherwise than undergo a veritable transformation, and if the work of the legislators at Cadiz was exotic and ill-digested, it nevertheless left certain traces on the history of Spain's political development. In order that this political growth might proceed in a natural channel to a change on constitutional lines it was eminently desirable that it should be put in accord with the traditions and convictions to which most Spaniards adhered, and such would have been the best course for Spain's national welfare and prosperity. But by proceeding otherwise the Cortes of Cadiz and the King paved the way for sanguinary civil strife, which was the basic cause of the paralysis of Spain's life and prosperity during the 19th century.

In proportion as the reforms introduced by the Liberals wounded feelings that were implanted deeply, the resistance of the opposers thereto was the more bitter and desperate. As such feelings on the part of those who adhered to tradition were not sagely directed by the King, so as to follow the natural political and evolutionary course which the times required, the retrograde element regarded the reformers, many of them well-intentioned though not always prudent, with no sentiment other than detestation, and held that their ideas should be combated by violence alone. On the other hand, the development in Spain of the system of guerrillas and small militant forces, as a means of opposing the veteran troops of Napoleon, constituted a bad training for times of peace, in that they were joined by those very soldiers of ours who had performed such fine achievements during the Peninsular War, but who now found in these small bodies a convenient instrument for disturbing political discipline. Thus began the series of *pronunciamientos* which, notwithstanding the victory of the Liberal cause in 1839, interrupted the smooth march of a well-ordered constitutional system until the restoration of the Monarchy in 1874.

Fortunately, however, during the last forty-five years those evils and the passions which gave rise to them, have passed from our memory. There is hardly a vestige left of the old Carlism, and its reappearance under arms is very improbable at any rate, as long as our monarchic institutions are preserved and no attack is made upon religious beliefs in our country.

The Constitutional Monarchy of Don Alfonso XIII has moreover destroyed those extremist parties which, under the republican flag, still existed during his father's reign. To-day they are no more than a shadow without substance, and it can be said with truth that the institutions of Spain are practically unquestioned. If other problems and dangers within the social order are not remote from the Spanish life of to-day, this is a difficulty which may be said to be relatively secondary. The trouble is one from which all civilised countries are suffering in a greater or less degree.

Milton Keynes UK
Ingram Content Group UK Ltd.
UKHW010709260923
429386UK00001B/3